Inside Eye

DINOSAURS
AND OTHER PREHISTORIC
CREATURES

Written by Margot Channing
Illustrated by Carolyn Scrace

CONTENTS

What is a Dinosaur?

Dinosaurs were a hugely varied group of reptiles. Some were no bigger than a dog, others were the length of four buses. They lived during the Mesozoic era of our planet's history, from 225 million years ago until 64 million years ago, before they suddenly died out. In the Mesozoic era, the Earth's landscape and climate often changed dramatically, and dinosaurs had to evolve to survive in these changing environments. Dinosaurs lived only on land.

Scientists examine dinosaur skeletons to find out more about these incredible creatures.

Many different types of dinosaur once walked on Earth.

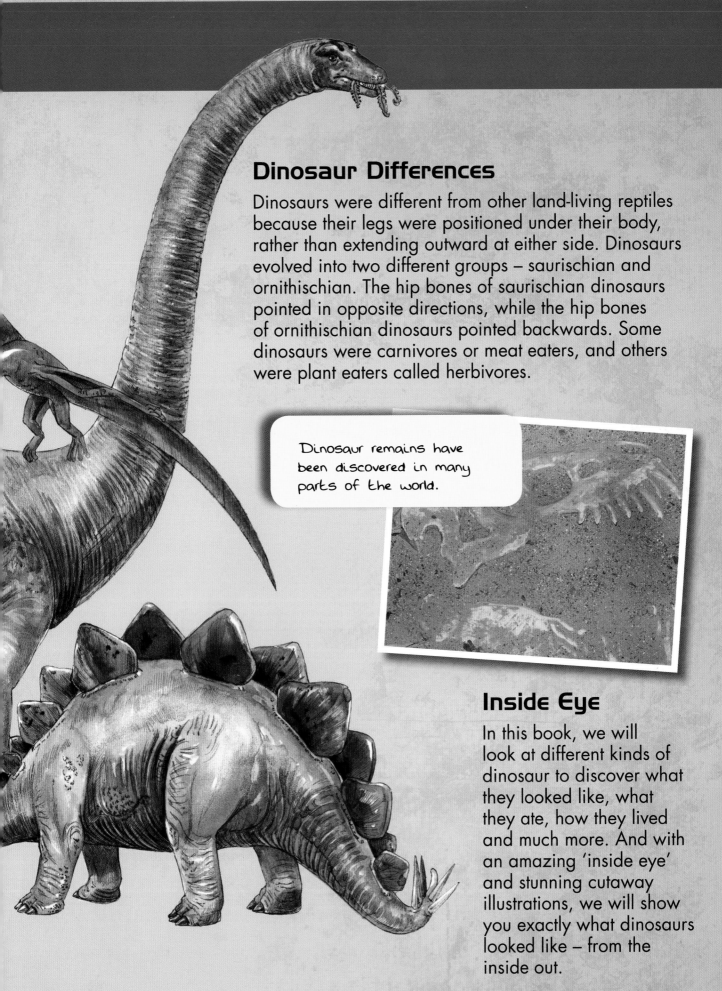

Dinosaur Differences

Dinosaurs were different from other land-living reptiles because their legs were positioned under their body, rather than extending outward at either side. Dinosaurs evolved into two different groups – saurischian and ornithischian. The hip bones of saurischian dinosaurs pointed in opposite directions, while the hip bones of ornithischian dinosaurs pointed backwards. Some dinosaurs were carnivores or meat eaters, and others were plant eaters called herbivores.

Dinosaur remains have been discovered in many parts of the world.

Inside Eye

In this book, we will look at different kinds of dinosaur to discover what they looked like, what they ate, how they lived and much more. And with an amazing 'inside eye' and stunning cutaway illustrations, we will show you exactly what dinosaurs looked like – from the inside out.

Dinosaur Age

Scientists usually split the Mesozoic era – the Age of the Dinosaurs – into three periods: the Triassic period (225 to 200 million years ago), the Jurassic period (200 to 135 million years ago) and the Cretaceous period (135 to 64 million years ago). Dinosaurs first appeared during the Triassic period and became the most dominant animals.

Time Spiral

This time spiral showing the Mesozoic era starts from the bottom up from the beginning of the Triassic period (225 million years ago), onwards through the Jurassic period (200 to 135 million years ago) and ends at the top with the Cretaceous period (64 million years ago).

Incredible Variety

Dinosaurs were of different shapes and sizes. Brachiosaurus was an amazing 27 m long. It was the heaviest dinosaur to ever live, weighing the same as 17 elephants: more than 80,000 kg. Much quicker and more nimble was the bird-like Avimimus, at just 1.5 m long.

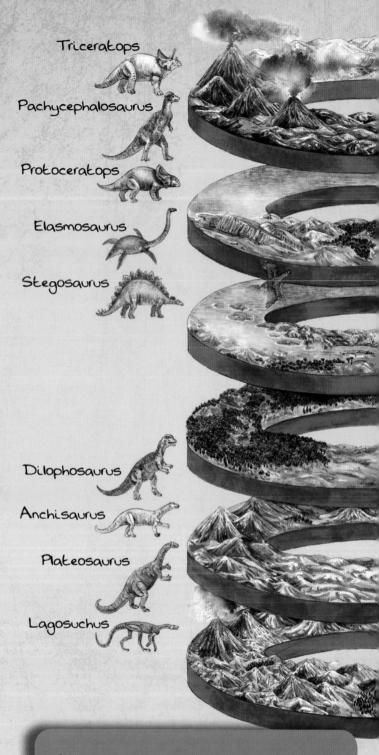

Triceratops

Pachycephalosaurus

Protoceratops

Elasmosaurus

Stegosaurus

Dilophosaurus

Anchisaurus

Plateosaurus

Lagosuchus

Alongside the time spiral are dinosaurs (not drawn to scale) that existed at that time. Flying around the middle of the spiral are two prehistoric reptiles, Eudimorphodon and Rhamphorhynchus, and the only known prehistoric bird, Archaeopteryx.

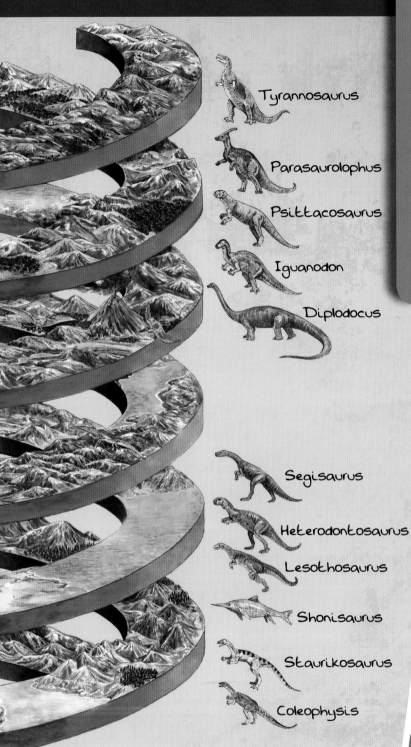

Tyrannosaurus

Parasaurolophus

Psittacosaurus

Iguanodon

Diplodocus

Segisaurus

Heterodontosaurus

Lesothosaurus

Shonisaurus

Staurikosaurus

Coleophysis

Cretaceous

Jurassic

Triassic

The first dinosaurs evolved in the Triassic period (bottom), then became abundant in the Jurassic period (middle). In the Cretaceous period (top), fish, flowering plants and birds evolved, but a mass extinction wiped the dinosaurs from the planet.

Changing World

When dinosaurs existed, many parts of the world that are now separated by the oceans were still joined together. Over millions of years, landmasses have moved apart and separated into the continents that we know today.

Dinosaur digs have taken place on every continent. Unearthed fossils show where certain types of dinosaurs lived on Earth and when they died. They also give us clues about dinosaurs' habits.

Killer Giants

Two distinct groups of carnivorous dinosaur evolved. They were called theropods, meaning they could walk on two feet. The first of these two groups appeared between 190 and 150 million years ago, during the Jurassic period, and included Dilophosaurus. Of the second group, which lived at the end of the Cretaceous period, between 75 and 64 million years ago, the most terrifying dinosaur was Tyrannosaurus.

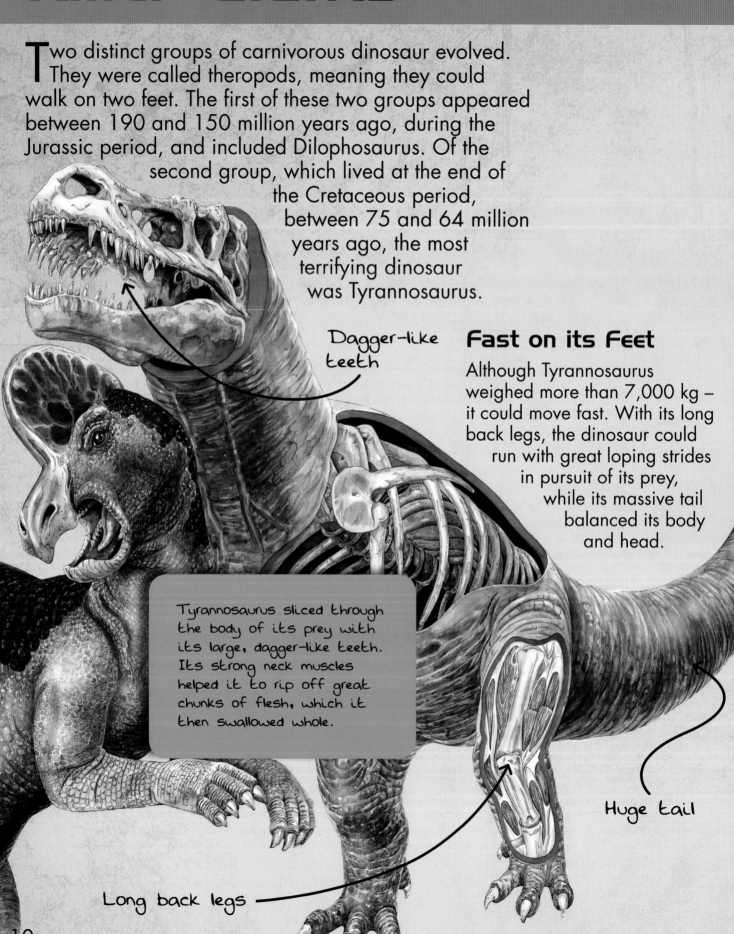

Dagger-like teeth

Fast on its Feet

Although Tyrannosaurus weighed more than 7,000 kg – it could move fast. With its long back legs, the dinosaur could run with great loping strides in pursuit of its prey, while its massive tail balanced its body and head.

Tyrannosaurus sliced through the body of its prey with its large, dagger-like teeth. Its strong neck muscles helped it to rip off great chunks of flesh, which it then swallowed whole.

Huge tail

Long back legs

Like Tyrannosaurus, Dilophosaurus was a fast mover. It had a kink in its upper jaw that it may have used to grip onto its prey. Modern crocodiles have the same kink.

First Big Meat Eater

Dilophosaurus was the earliest large carnivorous dinosaur, living 190 to 180 million years ago. It had a series of bony plates that formed a crest on its skull.

The skulls of all big carnivorous dinosaurs were formed from thick bone to withstand the jarring when the jaws were clamped shut. The skull bones included hollow areas to lighten the head so it was less heavy.

Mini Legs

A Tyrannosaurus' resting position was probably on its stomach, making it difficult for such a heavy creature to get up. The dinosaur may have used its tiny front legs as levers to balance itself when it rose from its resting position.

Resting

Standing up

Meat Eaters

Among the theropods were smaller, more nimble meat eaters, including Oviraptor, Deinonychus and Avimimus. They had lighter bodies and long muscular legs that allowed them to run fast over long distances. Deinonychus used this skill to chase other dinosaurs, while Avimimus caught insects. Oviraptor's diet probably contained eggs, shellfish and even some plants.

Attack of the Claw

Deinonychus had a huge 'terrible claw' on the second toe of each back foot. When the dinosaur ran, it raised the claw to protect the sharp point. When it attacked, the claw was lowered to slash open the belly of its prey.

Claw

The teeth of Deinonychus pointed backwards, which may have helped it to tear and chew its food.

Is it a Bird?

Feathers

Avimimus was a small, fast theropod that probably ate insects. It was not a bird but had bird-like features, such as a short skull, a beak with no teeth and possibly even some feathers, although experts cannot agree on this.

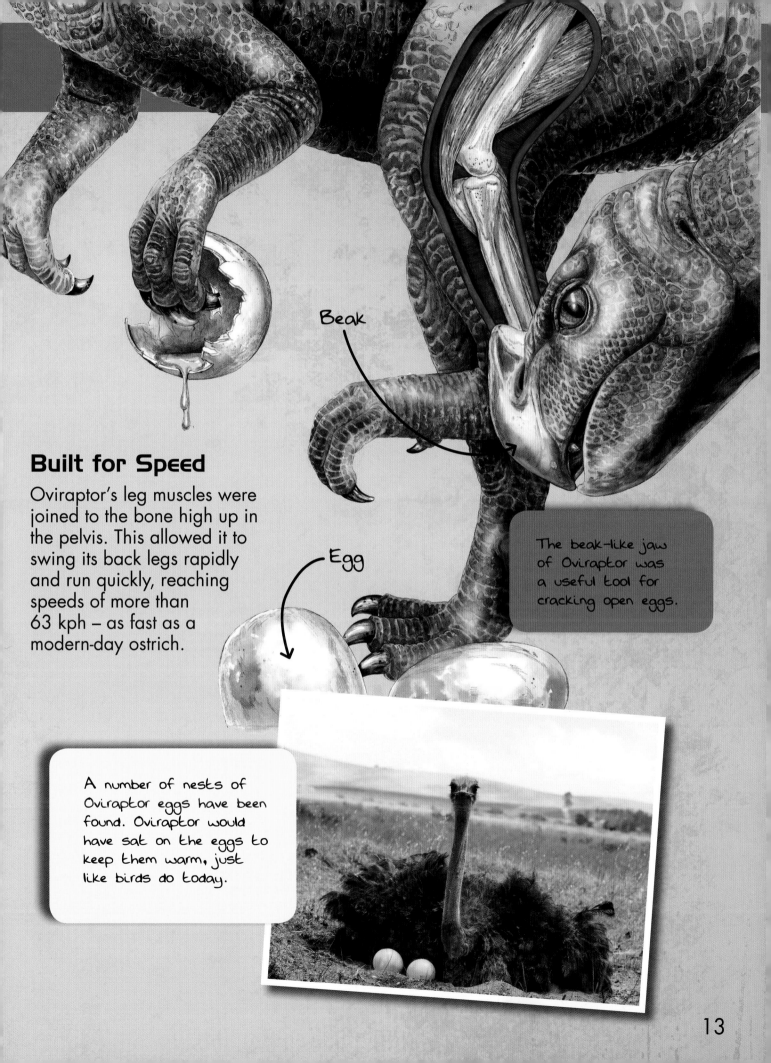

Beak

Built for Speed

Oviraptor's leg muscles were joined to the bone high up in the pelvis. This allowed it to swing its back legs rapidly and run quickly, reaching speeds of more than 63 kph – as fast as a modern-day ostrich.

Egg

The beak-like jaw of Oviraptor was a useful tool for cracking open eggs.

A number of nests of Oviraptor eggs have been found. Oviraptor would have sat on the eggs to keep them warm, just like birds do today.

Plant Eaters

All ornithischian dinosaurs were plant eaters, or herbivores. There were many changes in climate during the Mesozoic era, and herbivorous dinosaurs, such as Iguanodon, Dryosaurus, Heterodontosaurus and Psittacosaurus, had to adapt their diet to the changing availability of plants. Iguanodons, for example, developed more and larger teeth to cope with the tougher plants.

Iguanodon

An adult Iguanodon was about 10 m long and could stand and move around upright, balanced by its strong, supportive tail. It had small but sturdy front legs that allowed it to eat ground level plants and to rest on all fours. Iguanodon had a long snout with elongated jaws and ridged teeth that it used to grind and chew vegetation.

Thumb spike

Although Iguanodon was a slow-moving plant eater, it was fierce when attacked. It defended itself using a sharp thumb spike.

Strong front leg

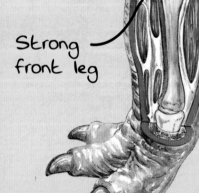

Parrot Face

Psittacosaurus, which lived between 98 and 90 million years ago, had a strong skull with a parrot-like beak. Its name means 'parrot lizard'. The beak was useful for tearing and slicing through vegetation.

Heterodontosaurus lived in the early Jurassic period, between 190 and 180 million years ago, when much of the Earth's surface was developing into humid, lush rainforest.

Quite a Mouthful

Heterodontosaurus means 'mixed-tooth reptile'. It was an unusual dinosaur because it had three types of teeth, when most dinosaurs had only one. It had sharp front teeth for cutting into plants, fangs at the side for breaking up bark and ridged back teeth for chewing.

During the Jurassic period, the developing rainforests provided excellent places for predators to lie in wait for passing prey.

Strong tail

Dinosaur Giants

The late Jurassic period, about 150 to 135 million years ago, was the age of the biggest dinosaurs, when Diplodocus and Brachiosaurus, both 27 m in length, roamed the landscape. All of the giant dinosaurs were herbivores and had to eat vast amounts of plant material to maintain their size. Their long necks easily stretched to the foliage at the tops of trees where smaller dinosaurs could not reach.

Heads Up

Brachiosaurus had a very long neck, measuring about 9 m. Like other long-necked dinosaurs, it may have had as many as eight hearts to pump blood up to its brain. There may have been two main hearts in the chest and three smaller paired hearts in the neck itself.

Brachiosaurus

The neck vertebrae of Brachiosaurus had to be very large to support the length of the dinosaur's neck. Its skull bones, however, were quite thin to reduce the weight of its head.

Out of Proportion

The skull of Diplodocus was tiny compared with the rest of its body. It had a long, broad snout with narrow, pointed teeth that it used to cut through leaves and branches. The eyes were set quite far back in the head and the nostrils were on top, almost between the eyes.

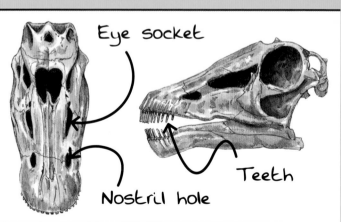

Eye socket

Nostril hole

Teeth

Unusual Nostrils

Camarasaurus lived 150 to 125 million years ago. It had a short, square skull with a wide nose, and its nostrils were on the top of its head, although the reason for this is unknown. This plant-eating dinosaur used its rows of thick, spoon-like teeth to strip the leaves from trees and shrubs.

Camarasaurus

At 18 m long, Camarasaurus was smaller than Brachiosaurus but similar in body shape.

The well-preserved Diplodocus in the main hall of the Natural History Museum in London is perhaps the best-known dinosaur skeleton in the world. It has stood in the museum since 1905.

17

Smallest Dinosaurs

A number of small dinosaurs, both herbivores and carnivores, emerged in the early and late Jurassic period. There is controversy over whether these dinosaurs were cold-blooded, like the reptiles of today, or warm-blooded like the mammals and birds of today. Did small dinosaurs store up body heat in the way that crocodiles do, or did some evolve to become warm-blooded, giving rise to the ancestors of modern birds?

Compsognathus' strong and flexible neck meant it could make rapid, sudden movements with its head, which helped it to catch fast-moving prey.

Delicate jaw

Lightweight Sprinter

Compsognathus was one of the smallest dinosaurs that ever lived. The name Compsognathus means 'pretty jaw' and this dinosaur certainly had very delicate skull bones. Its jaws were long and slender and each had a row of sharp, pointed teeth. Compsognathus must have had quick reactions and good eyesight to catch prey such as fast-moving lizards and large insects.

Compsognathus grew to a length of 70 cm and weighed no more than a large turkey. Its light skeleton and long, thin back legs made it a fast runner.

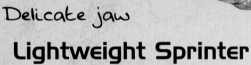

Not So Little Plant Eater

The smallest dinosaur skeleton ever found was a Mussaurus, measuring 20 cm from head to tail. It was found in Argentina in the 1970s and named 'mouse lizard' because of its tiny size. It is now known that this was only a newly hatched dinosaur that might grow to 3 m in length – bigger than any mouse!

Mussaurus

Lightweight skeleton

How Many Fingers?

The number of digits, or fingers, on a dinosaur's front feet varied between one and five. Compsognathus had only two digits of useful size, with a third 'reduced' digit that had no function. Some experts think Compsognathus used its feet to grip prey.

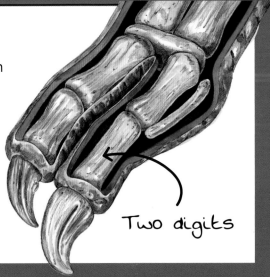

Two digits

Armour Plated

Many dinosaurs, such as Parasaurolophus and Triceratops, had elaborately shaped skulls, with crests or horns. Others, such as Stegosaurus, had rows of bony plates along their back. This armour was more than just protection for these big, slow plant eaters. It may also have helped them to smell, communicate or keep cool.

Parasaurolophus may also have used its crest in courting rituals to attract and keep a mate.

Crest

Strange Headgear

Parasaurolophus, which lived between 76 and 74 million years ago, was part of a group of dinosaurs called the hadrosaurs that all had distinctive crests or spikes on their head. Parasaurolophus probably used its long, tube-like crest as a way of making its call sound louder.

This is a model of stegosaurus. Stegosaurus lived 150 to 140 million years ago. The bony plates on its back had a rich supply of blood vessels, which allowed the dinosaur to store heat and control body temperature.

Bit of a Big Head

Triceratops, which lived between 72 and 64 million years ago, weighed about 5,400 kg and grew to a length of 9 m. It had two huge horns and one smaller horn. Triceratops had a neck frill ribbed with bony spines and a massive skull that ended in a horny beak, which was used to clip off tough vegetation.

The head of a Triceratops was huge – quite out of proportion with the rest of its body. In an adult, the head alone took up almost a quarter of the dinosaur's length.

Neck frill

Horn

Beak

Duck Faces

Hadrosaurs were some of the oddest-looking dinosaurs. The name of the family means 'duck-billed dinosaurs', which comes from the similarity between the head of a hadrosaur and that of a modern duck.

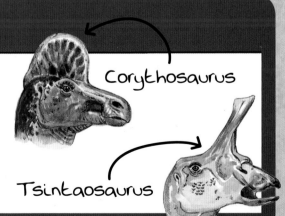

Corythosaurus

Tsintaosaurus

Reproduction

Dinosaurs reproduced by laying eggs. They laid them mostly in hard-to-reach places on high ground. The pointed end of each egg faced inwards, towards the centre of the nest, to make sure that the rounded end of the egg, from which the baby dinosaurs emerged, was not blocked.

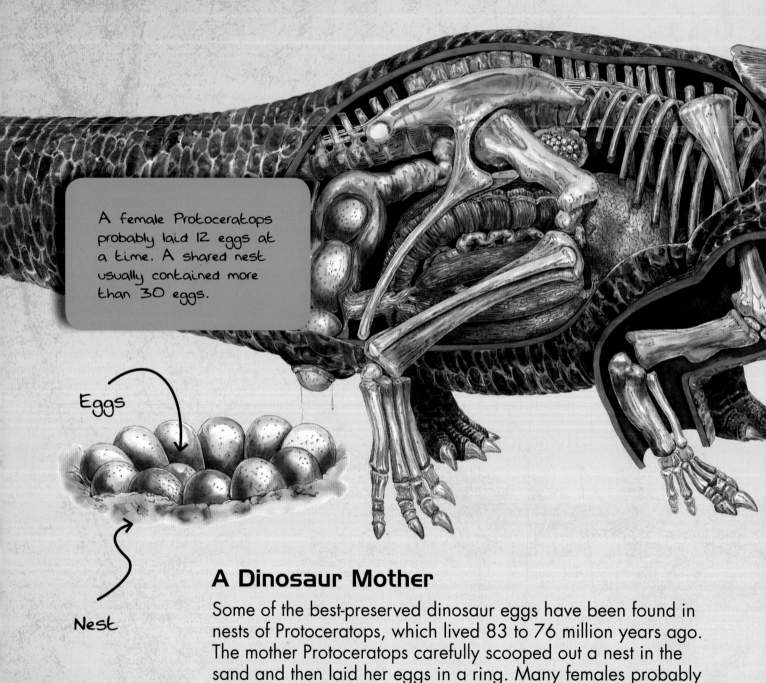

A female Protoceratops probably laid 12 eggs at a time. A shared nest usually contained more than 30 eggs.

Eggs

Nest

A Dinosaur Mother

Some of the best-preserved dinosaur eggs have been found in nests of Protoceratops, which lived 83 to 76 million years ago. The mother Protoceratops carefully scooped out a nest in the sand and then laid her eggs in a ring. Many females probably used the same breeding ground and may have taken turns to incubate the eggs and share the care of the babies.

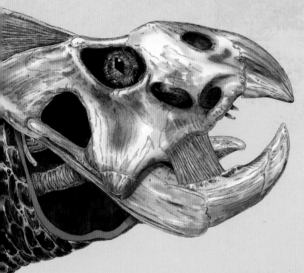

Working Together

The nesting habits of Maiasaura, a dinosaur that lived 80 to 64 million years ago, show that dinosaurs could be very sociable animals. While some females dug new nests, others that had already laid eggs would turn their eggs and make neccessary repairs to nests.

Inside the Egg

Like the egg of a modern bird, a dinosaur egg had a tough protective shell. It contained a cushion of fluid to keep the developing baby, or embryo, safe from injury as the egg was turned in the nest.

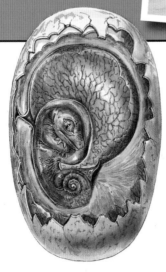

This is the skeleton of Protoceratops. An expedition to the Gobi Desert in Mongolia in the 1920s discovered nests of unhatched Protoceratops eggs. Each egg was around 16 cm long.

Dinosaur Defence

The world of the dinosaurs was a violent place. Different groups of dinosaurs struggled against each other for survival in the changing Mesozoic landscape. Whether protecting themselves from attack by fierce predators like Tyrannosaurus or fighting for their territory, dinosaurs devised many different kinds of defence.

Spiky Opponent

The thick, bony plates in the leathery skin of Euoplocephalus helped it to withstand attacks by Albertosaurus 75 to 64 million years ago. The Euoplocephalus had pointed spines on its head and along its back that could easily wound a predator, and a heavy blow from its tail club could lame a persistent Albertosaurus or even knock it to the ground.

The large, round club at the end of Euoplocephalus' tail was an excellent weapon against predators. One sharp strike could inflict serious injury.

Euoplocephalus' club-like tail

On the Attack!

Some vulnerable plant-eating dinosaurs could be aggressive when threatened by a predator. Iguanodon had a dagger-like claw that could easily tear open a predator's neck muscles. A charging Triceratops, its horns bristling, was more than a match for a Tyrannosaurus.

Iguanodon's dagger-like claw

Charging Triceratops

Hylaeosaurus, when attacked, lay as flat as it could, exposing only its heavy armour and sharp spikes. Parasaurolophus may have escaped large predators by plunging into a river or lake to swim to safety.

Hylaeosaurus

Parasaurolophus

Albertosaurus

Survival Strategies

Different dinosaurs used different tactics to escape from or survive an attack. Some relied on tough body armour and fearsome spikes to deter or injure a predator, and others would group together to form a defensive cluster. Some smaller dinosaurs used the simplest strategy: running away as fast as they could from bigger, slower carnivores.

Euoplocephalus' tail club was an amazing structure. It was formed from bony plates that had fused together at the end of its tail. An adult tail club was 40 cm long, 61 cm wide and weighed around 4 kg.

Dinosaur End

No one knows for certain why dinosaurs became extinct at the end of the Cretaceous period, 64 million years ago. Many scientists believe that it was the result of a huge meteor, about the size of the Isle of Wight, hitting the Earth. This would have caused a massive cloud of debris to cover the planet, cutting out sunlight and bringing dramatic changes in climate. Dinosaurs died, while some mammals, lizards and snakes managed to survive.

Massive Impact

According to scientists, the meteor hit the Earth 20 times faster than a speeding bullet. It would have caused an enormous explosion as it began to vaporise in the Earth's atmosphere before colliding with the planet.

The impact of hitting the Earth changed the meteor from a solid object about 15 km wide into a huge cloud of dust and water vapour. Huge fires, earthquakes and tsunamis soon followed.

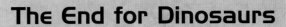

The End for Dinosaurs

After the impact of the meteor, darkness reigned for many months as sunlight, vital to plant growth, was completely blocked out. Clouds full of toxic gases choked the planet. Plants died instantly, leaving plant-eating dinosaurs without food. When the plant eaters died, meat-eating dinosaurs had nothing left to eat, and they, too, began to die out.

When the cloud eventually lifted, weak sunlight revealed a bleak and barren landscape with no plants and little sign of life. Tiny mammals survived by scavenging for food and eating insects.

The Earth is dotted with huge craters caused by meteors. The biggest, the Vredefort crater in South Africa, is 300 km wide and dates from 2,000 million years ago. Many scientists believe that the 180-km-wide Chicxulub crater, buried under the Yucatán Peninsula in Mexico, marks the point of impact of the meteor that wiped out the dinosaurs.

A meteor crater

Amazing Dino Facts

Big Killer

Tyrannosaurus was one of the largest carnivorous dinosaurs that ever lived. It was 12 m long, 5 m high and weighed over 7,000 kg.

Food Blender

The stomach of giant plant-eating dinosaurs, such as Diplodocus and Brachiosaurus, is thought to have contained a large number of stones. These gastroliths, meaning 'stomach stones', were used to grind branches, twigs and leaves into an easily digestible pulp.

Head to Head

Some dinosaurs attacked members of their own group. Pachycephalosaurus engaged in head-butting contests to decide which male was dominant.

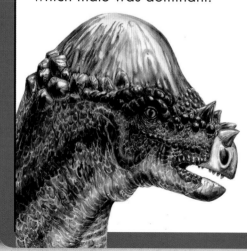

Riot of Colour

Dinosaurs are often shown as being dull grey or brown. In fact, just like reptiles today, they probably had a variety of skin colours. Pachycephalosaurus, for example, may have been brightly coloured, partly to attract a mate.

Iguano-wrong!

Rebuilding a dinosaur skeleton is difficult because the bones are often scattered and incomplete. Today's view of Iguanodon looks very different from the model made for the Great Exhibition of 1851 in London, which was the wrong shape and put the dinosaur's thumb spike on its nose!

Small Brain

The brains of many dinosaurs were tiny. An adult Stegosaurus might have weighed more than 1,500 kg but its brain was no bigger than a walnut and weighed less than 70–80 g.

Other Creatures

Dinosaurs were not the only animals to live on Earth during the Mesozoic era. Flying reptiles, early birds and ocean-living creatures all shared the planet at the same time.

Last of the Sun

When the meteor that brought the dinosaur age to an end hit the Earth, the last thing the dinosaurs would have seen before being plunged into darkness were the dramatic and colourful sunsets caused by dust from the impact.

Glossary

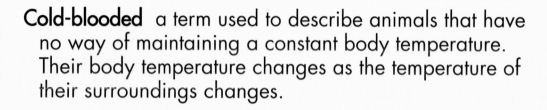

Ancestor an animal from which another animal is descended.

Carnivore an animal that eats meat.

Cold-blooded a term used to describe animals that have no way of maintaining a constant body temperature. Their body temperature changes as the temperature of their surroundings changes.

Cretaceous period the third period of the Mesozoic era, which lasted from 135 to 64 million years ago.

Digit a finger or toe.

Dominant a term used to describe an animal or group of animals that is the most important and/or the most abundant in an environment.

Evolved changed over a long period of time.

Extinction when all members of a group of plants or animals are dead.

Fossil the preserved remains of something that was once alive. Fossils are usually formed when a dead animal or plant is buried and then compressed by the weight of whatever had buried it.

Jurassic period the second period of the Mesozoic era, which lasted from 200 to 135 million years ago.

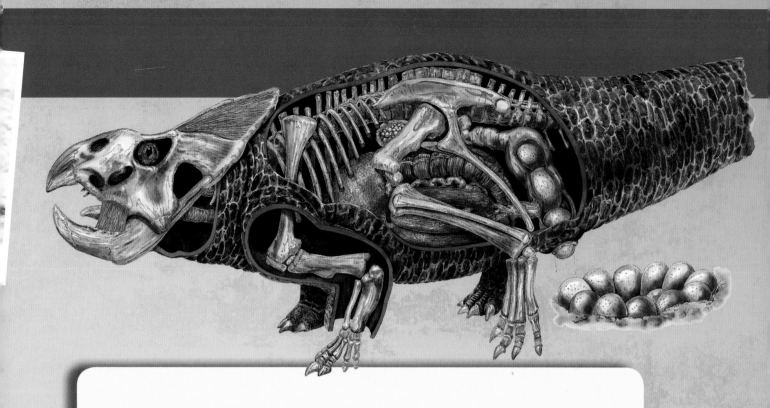

Mammals a group of warm-blooded animals that produce milk to feed their young and that have fur or hair.

Predator an animal that catches other animals for food.

Prey an animal that is, or may be, eaten by another.

Reptiles a group of cold-blooded animals that includes snakes, lizards, crocodiles, turtles, tortoises and the now-extinct dinosaurs.

Territory an area of land where an animal, or group of animals, lives.

Triassic period the first period of the Mesozoic era, which lasted from 225 to 200 million years ago.

Warm-blooded a term used to describe animals that can maintain the same body temperature, even when the surrounding temperature changes.

Index